Our Lady's Picture Book

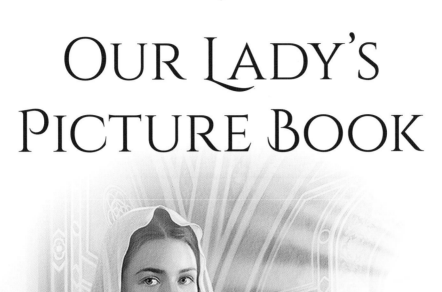

Anthony DeStefano
Illustrated by Juliana Kolesova

SOPHIA INSTITUTE PRESS
Manchester, NH

SOPHIA
INSTITUTE PRESS

Text Copyright © 2020 by Anthony DeStefano
Images Copyright © 2020 by Juliana Kolesova

Printed in the United States of America.

Sophia Institute Press®
Box 5284, Manchester, NH 03108
1-800-888-9344

www.SophiaInstitute.com
Sophia Institute Press® is a registered trademark of Sophia Institute.

ISBN: 978-1-64413-390-3

Library of Congress Control Number: 9781644133903

This book is dedicated to
Our Lady of Lourdes.
—*Anthony DeStefano*

Pictures help remind us of the people that we love;
People here on earth with us and Heaven up above.

Throughout the years Our Lady has been shown in many ways:
In paintings, statues, books and cards, and holiday displays.

These images can help us pray and make us faithful too.
From Our Lady's picture book, here are just a few...

When Jesus was a tiny tot
Our Lady got Him dressed.
She took Him to the Temple so
the Baby could be blessed.

Then Mary turned and saw a man,
faithful, wise, and old.
He told her she would suffer and
a sword would pierce her soul.

And sure enough, the man was right,
    and what he said came true.
Mary's life was very hard
    and full of sorrows too.

So when you're feeling sad and blue
    and gloomy now and then,
ask Our Lady for her help
    to make you smile again.

OUR LADY OF SORROWS

When Jesus was a little boy
    He had a scary dream.
He saw a cross and spear and nails
    and woke up with a scream.

His mother took Him in her arms
    and hugged and squeezed Him tight.
She kissed His head and held His hands
    and soon He felt all right.

So when you're scared and filled with fear
    and don't know what to do,
ask Our Lady for her help
    and she will comfort you.

OUR LADY OF PERPETUAL HELP

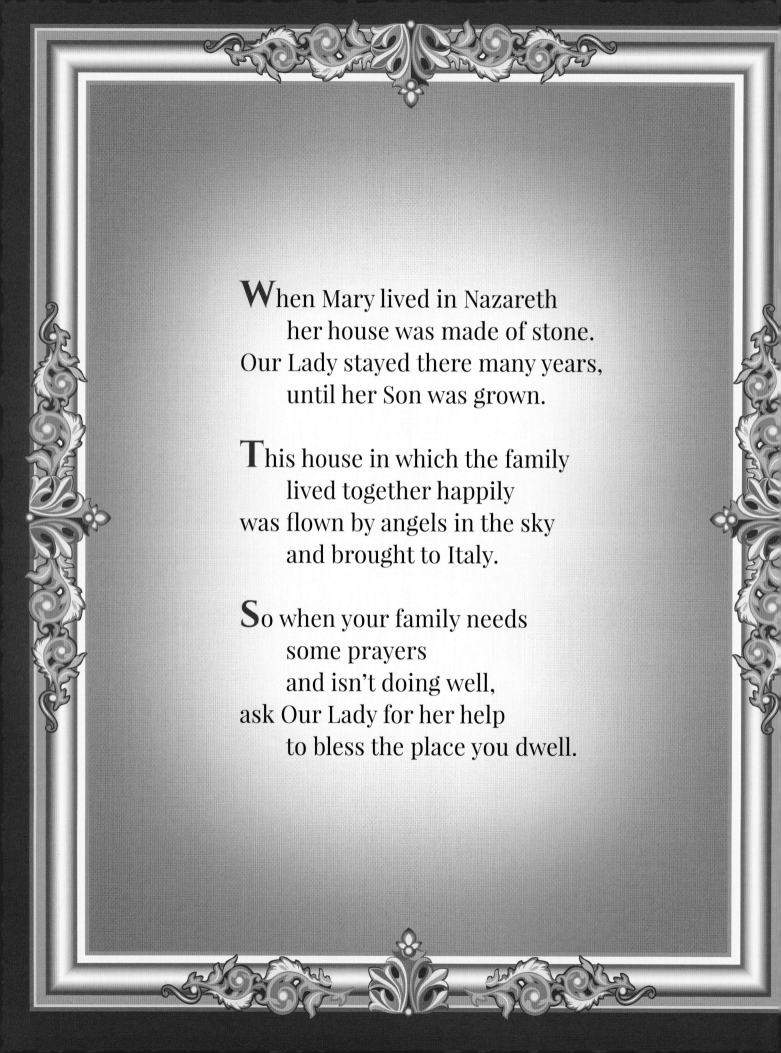

When Mary lived in Nazareth
    her house was made of stone.
Our Lady stayed there many years,
    until her Son was grown.

This house in which the family
    lived together happily
was flown by angels in the sky
    and brought to Italy.

So when your family needs
    some prayers
    and isn't doing well,
ask Our Lady for her help
    to bless the place you dwell.

OUR LADY OF LORETO

When Mary's mission was complete
and all her work was done,
her soul and body God took up
to be beside her Son.

From Heaven she can help us more
with constant, loving prayer,
sending graces down to us
and people everywhere.

So when your body's feeling weak
and sluggish, sick and sore,
ask Our Lady for her help
to make you strong and pure.

OUR LADY OF THE ASSUMPTION

When ships at sea are caught
    in storms and black clouds
    fill the night,
Our Lady leads them to the shore
    just like a guiding light.

She's often called the Northern Star
    because she points the way
to safety in the arms of Jesus
    when we go astray.

So when you're lost and in distress
    and feeling all alone,
ask Our Lady for her help,
    and she will lead you home.

OUR LADY, STAR OF THE SEA

When Christian people on the earth throughout their history were persecuted for their Faith they prayed the Rosary.

And when these Christians had to fight in battles on the sea,
Our Lady helped them with her prayers and gave them victory.

So when you're feeling overwhelmed
and trying not to sin,
ask Our Lady for her help
to struggle till you win.

OUR LADY OF THE ROSARY

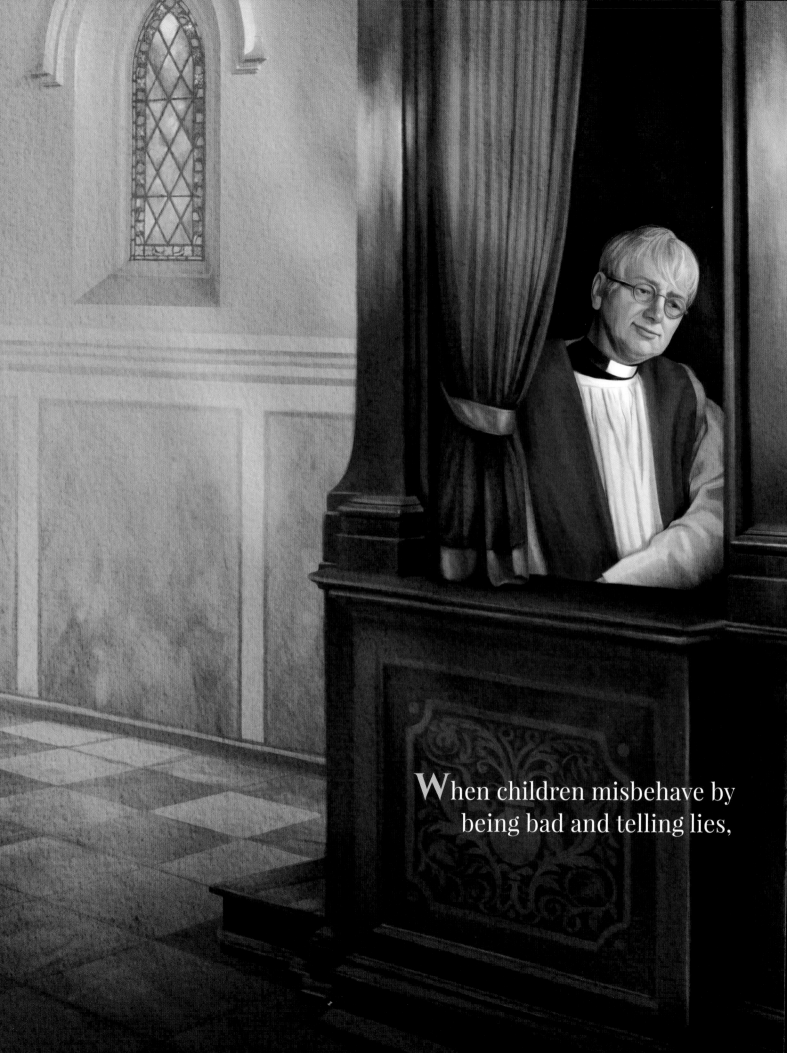

When children misbehave by
being bad and telling lies,

God forgives them always
if they just apologize.

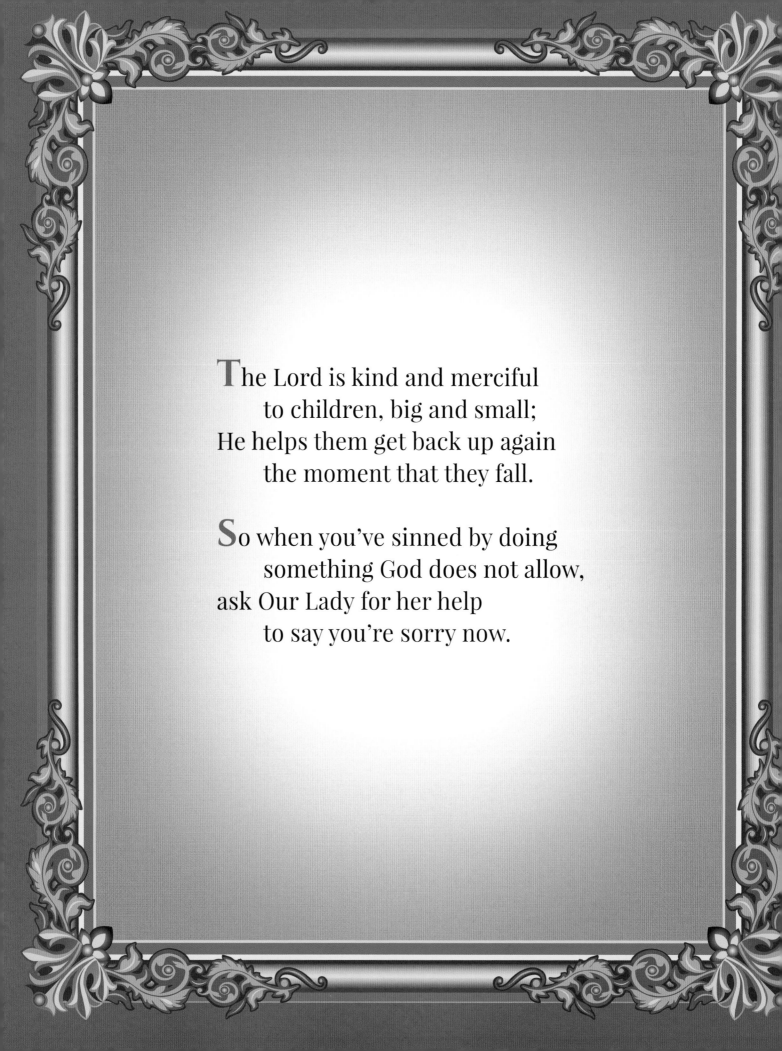

The Lord is kind and merciful
to children, big and small;
He helps them get back up again
the moment that they fall.

So when you've sinned by doing
something God does not allow,
ask Our Lady for her help
to say you're sorry now.

OUR LADY, MOTHER OF MERCY

When all the world is plagued by wars and hatred fills the air,

Mary prays to God for peace and friendship everywhere.

The only way the gift of peace
      can ever be restored
is if we worship Mary's Son,
      Jesus Christ the Lord.

So when you're feeling really mad
      at people that you know,
ask Our Lady for her help
      to let your anger go.

OUR LADY, QUEEN OF PEACE

Our Lady's heart belongs to God;
    it's spotless, clean, and pure.
That's why it's called "immaculate"
    for now and evermore.

Her heart in Heaven beats with love
    for boys and girls like you.
She's mother to Our Lord above
    —but she's *your* mother too!

So ask Our Lady for her help;
    ask her day and night.
Ask her when you're feeling sad;
    ask with all your might!

Ask Our Lady, never fear!
    Ask for anything.
She will bring you peace and joy
    from Jesus Christ the King!

THE IMMACULATE HEART OF MARY

From the Bible

"And the angel said to [Mary], 'The Holy Spirit will come upon you, and the power of the Most High will overshadow you; therefore the child to be born will be called holy, the Son of God.'"

— *Luke 1:35*

"And Elizabeth was filled with the Holy Spirit and she exclaimed with a loud cry, 'Blessed are you among women, and blessed is the fruit of your womb!'…. And Mary said, 'My soul magnifies the Lord, and my spirit rejoices in God my Savior…. For behold, henceforth all generations will call me blessed;'"

— *Luke 1:41, 42, 46–48*

"There was a marriage at Cana in Galilee, and the mother of Jesus was there…His mother said to the servants, 'Do whatever he tells you.'"

— *John 2:1, 5*

"When Jesus saw his mother, and the disciple whom he loved standing near, he said to his mother, 'Woman, behold, your son!' Then he said to the disciple, 'Behold, your mother!' And from that hour the disciple took her to his own home."

— *John 19:26–27*

(Revised Standard Version, Catholic Edition)

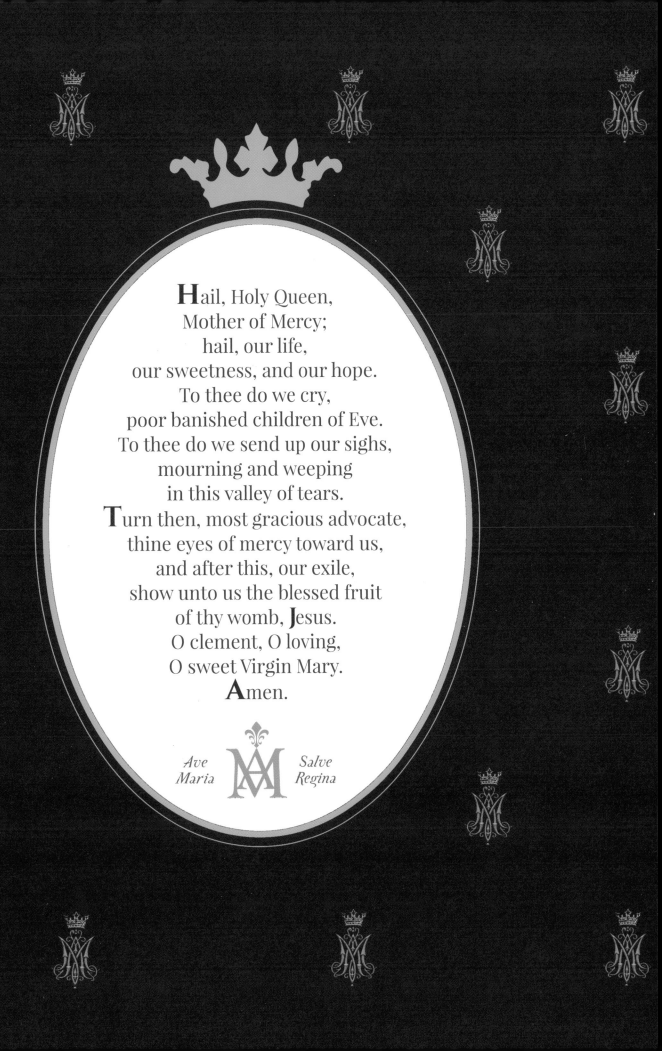

Hail, Holy Queen,
Mother of Mercy;
hail, our life,
our sweetness, and our hope.
To thee do we cry,
poor banished children of Eve.
To thee do we send up our sighs,
mourning and weeping
in this valley of tears.
Turn then, most gracious advocate,
thine eyes of mercy toward us,
and after this, our exile,
show unto us the blessed fruit
of thy womb, **J**esus.
O clement, O loving,
O sweet Virgin Mary.
Amen.

*Ave
Maria*

*Salve
Regina*